Transformational Grief
IN THE BOOK OF JOB

General Conference
July 25, 2024

Transformational Grief
IN THE BOOK OF JOB

Blessings Kimberly Nicklu

Loretta F. Baker

Dr. Loretta Baker

XULON ELITE

Xulon Press Elite
2301 Lucien Way #415
Maitland, FL 32751
407.339.4217
www.xulonpress.com

Paperback ISBN-13: 978-1-66287-535-9
Hard Cover ISBN-13: 978-1-66287-536-6
Ebook ISBN-13: 978-1-66287-537-3

Dedication

To:

My Mother
My Husband
My Older Daughter & Her Husband
My Younger Daughter & Her Husband
My Only Grandson

Table of Contents

List of Abbreviations

MSG Eugene Peterson's *The Message*

NIV New International Version

NLT New Living Translation

Preface

"When doubts filled my mind, your comfort
gave me renewed hope and cheer."
Ps. 94:19, NLT

I give all praise and glory to the name of Jesus the Christ, my Lord and Savior, who extended to me the grace to complete the project that is the basis for this publication.

I thank all generations of my family, my husband, our daughters, our grandson, and sons-in-law, who encouraged me to keep going when it appeared I was stuck. My husband deserves special gratitude for his dependable love and invaluable technical and administrative expertise. He provided everything I needed at just the right times.

I appreciate the members of First Gethsemane Baptist Church and the interim pastor, Rev. Keith A. Bush, Sr., for their perseverance and participation after the death of Dr. T. Vaughn Walker, who served them as pastor for nearly 35 years. Dr. Walker inspired me to bring a coherent structure to my call to grief ministry through pursuing the Doctor of Ministry. He served as my first faculty supervisor at The Southern Baptist Theological Seminary. Even in his last days, he continued to encourage my soul.

I thank the Taylortown African Methodist Episcopal Zion Church family and their pastor, Presiding Elder Erich Von Shumake, where I served as Minister of Music while completing my doctoral project. They played major roles in bringing that project to fruition.

Finally, I thank Dr. Shane W. Parker for graciously agreeing to supervise me after Dr. Walker's death. I am grateful to all who loved me, cared for me, prayed for me, and helped me along the way.

Loretta Faye Baker

Grieving Can Help Us

*"So be truly glad. There is wonderful joy ahead, even though you
must endure many trials for a little while." 1 Pet. 1:6, NLT*

On March 6, 2020, I was watching television when my cell phone
rang. It was a call from my mother's brother — but not the one
who was her primary caregiver. My uncle told me that he found my life-
less mother in her home after her friends were unable to reach her by
phone. Suddenly, death made its way through the door of my heart and
broke it. She was eight months away from her 90th birthday on November
1. She worked for 43 years in a hospital owned and operated by the
Catholic Church. As a proud Baptist, she bragged to everyone about her
special blessing for having been born on All Saints Day. My daughters
and I were making plans to celebrate my mother's birthday because we
wanted to honor her and thank her for blessing us with her spiritual gift
of giving.

My husband and I left Louisville, Kentucky and drove to Fort Worth,
Texas to make final arrangements. At the same time, all media outlets
reported that a deadly virus was spreading rapidly. In less than 10 days
after we received the life-changing phone call about my mother, businesses
and churches closed until further notice. Her visitation, funeral, and the

fellowship meal afterward were sparsely attended out of an abundance of caution. Her home going service on March 16, 2020 was the last in person worship at that church for several months.

Hotels, restaurants, and service stations started closing. We had to check out of the hotel much earlier than scheduled. We were one of the last four families to leave the hotel. On our way home, truck stops with drive through pick up for fast food were our only options. We were afraid to stop for bathroom breaks as we drove more than 13 hours from Fort Worth to Louisville.

Relieved to be home, we were not prepared for toilet paper, thermometer, and face mask shortages. Lawyers closed their offices and judges did not hold court. As a result, our plans for probate had to change. Sometimes change is imposed on us without our input. Other times, we choose to change in order to get the best outcome.

I taught classes about change. I researched grief and change. I earned a Doctor of Ministry by completing a project on grief and change. However, experiencing grief and change during a pandemic gave me a chance to practice what I taught. I am convinced that during more than 2 years of grief aversion, grief deflection, and grief introspection, I was being transformed. I know that I am changed because I am no longer *going to publish* a book that helps develop grief care skills. Now *I am doing it.*

With participation from First Gethsemane Baptist Church from Louisville, Kentucky and the Kentucky Annual Conference of African Methodist Episcopal Zion Church, I administered a survey about grief to assess the knowledge and understanding of grief among their members and Annual Conference attendees. The results indicated respondents welcomed the opportunity to learn more about grief. We worked together to learn how grief could be transformative; how to promote grief self-care; and how to encourage grief care for one another. I pray that this offering provides similar blessings and lessons.

Prologue

"He comforts us in all our troubles so that we can comfort others. When they are troubled, we will be able to give them the same comfort God has given us." 2 Cor. 1:4, NLT

I realized that grievers who needed support weeks and months following losses were usually referred to resources outside the church. In doing so, the church outsourced grief care to social and behavioral health agencies. Any reference to religion is specifically prohibited in some grief programs to avoid the appearance of proselytizing. Church members and their families who participated in grief counseling did not receive grief care that incorporated examples of how persons in the Bible worked through their grief.

You can read in 2 Corinthians 1:3-7 where Paul told the entire church how important it was for them to comfort one another. They were to use biblical examples along with personal experiences to help one another in times of trouble. In addition to having physical needs met, compassion and comfort provided a spiritual connection to the healing and restorative love of God.

Interestingly, grievers tend to deny their need for help. They almost instinctively declare their wellness by saying, "I am okay." However, those in mourning are often very receptive to securing help for others. Parishioners acknowledged they lacked the confidence and felt they were not equipped to care for grievers. Skilled caregivers understand the scope of loss and have the ability to recognize grief. Learning to manage their own grief is important in ministry to others. Anxious parishioners often misused Scripture or quoted verses that were inappropriate for the situation in an attempt to demonstrate unshakable faith and spiritual depth. As a result, Christians could appear cold and detached.

Grief and loss are recurring biblical themes that Christians tend to avoid or gloss over. Scripture provides examples of many who suffered and experienced loss. This study will examine grief and suffering in the book of Job to show how he and his friends grew in their knowledge and understanding of God's character. I will introduce the principles that form *A Theory of Grief* and show how Job was transformed as he coped with crises and conflict, considered the consolation from his friends, and confronted the internal and external attacks on his faith in the Lord. You will see how grieving helped change the way Job and his friends thought about troubles, trials, and tests.

Grieving can help us let go, focus forward, press on, reach for the future, and grab hold of unimagined possibilities. I hope you can employ the principles in *A Theory of Grief* to help you learn God's will and trust that His plans for you are good, pleasing, and perfect. Ultimately, I pray that as you care for yourselves, you will arise, mobilize, and organize as grief caregivers to bless others who mourn. "Dear friend, I pray that you may enjoy good health and that all may go well with you, even as your soul is getting along well." (3 Jn. 1:2, NIV)

CHAPTER 1

Grief Matters

"I consider that our present sufferings are not worth comparing with the glory that will be revealed in us." Rom. 8:18, NIV

In the book *Changing for Good*, James O. Prochaska, John C. Norcross, and Carlo C. DiClemente open by stating the obvious, "Welcome or not, change is unavoidable."[1] They go on to say, "Few of the changes we experience are under our control: When we watch the often tragic history of the world unfold or face our personal tragedies, we feel helpless, or at least limited as to what we can do."[2] I have concluded that change is unstoppable, irreversible, and impossible to ignore. Once changed, there is no going back. The moment passed. The moment is lost and cannot be recovered. The authors explain that Stages of Change are available as tools for behavior modification when someone *chooses* to change an aspect of their lives. Examples include people who want to stop smoking, break addictions, or lose weight.

---

[1] James O. Prochaska, John C. Norcross, and Carlo C. DiClemente, *Changing for Good* (New York: Harper Collins, 2006), 13.

[2] Ibid.

1

There are times when we pray for change. In the Old Testament war between Israel and the Amorites, Joshua prayed. "So the sun stood still and the moon stayed in place until the nation of Israel had defeated its enemies." (Josh. 10:13a, NLT) Even though *time* stood still, events kept going until the relationship between nations had changed. Change was unstoppable. We find in Isaiah 38:5-8 that the Lord interceded for Hezekiah and caused time to move in reverse. The sundial moved backward but Hezekiah's date of death moved forward by 15 years. Israel and Hezekiah experienced change.

Deciding to take steps that lead to positive outcomes and improve the quality of life is admirable. Contentment can cause us to resist change. However, there are times when change forces its way into our lives. Whether by accident or on purpose, crises can bring suffering, loss, and grief.

Nothing changes a person like trouble. It is hard to imagine how Job felt as he received one message after another — each more devastating than the one still being reported. The last messenger detailed what took place as *all* of his children lost their lives. He had the nearly universal normal and natural, physical and emotional response to his trouble. Job did not hide his grief. He mourned. That is one way to accept overwhelming, unavoidable, and uncontrollable losses that could leave you feeling helpless. "Dear brothers and sisters, when troubles of any kind come your way, consider it an opportunity for great joy." (James 1:2, NLT) Just like the Lord showed himself mighty and strong for Israel and was merciful to Hezekiah, grieving can help you move from one condition to another — from mourning to morning; from broken to blessed; from ashes to beauty; and from being overwhelmed by a sense of despair to prevailing with the power of praise.

In *Comfort the Grieving: Ministering God's Grace in Times of Loss* Paul Tautges wrote, "Grief is part of the human experience, a reflection of our being created in God's image."[3] Periods of mourning allow opportunities to adjust to changes that result from loss. Mourning took many forms in Scripture. When Jacob heard that Joseph was dead, he was distraught and purposed to mourn until his own death. Several years later he learned that Joseph was alive. After Jacob died, we see what happened, "Then Joseph directed the physicians in his service to embalm his father Israel. So the physicians embalmed him, taking a full forty days, for that was the time required for embalming. And the Egyptians mourned for him seventy days." (Gen. 50:2-3, NIV) Following an elaborate ceremony we read, "When they reached the threshing floor of Atad, near the Jordan, they lamented loudly and bitterly; and there Joseph observed a seven-day period of mourning for his father." (Gen. 50:10, NIV)

According to Deuteronomy 34:8, "The Israelites grieved for Moses in the plains of Moab thirty days, until the time of weeping and mourning was over." On the other hand, David mourned a portion of only one day after learning that King Saul and his son were killed in 2 Samuel 1:12. Sometime people tore their clothes in addition to putting on sackcloth and sitting in ashes. Isaiah let the Israelites know that the Lord cared about them when he wrote:

> "The Spirit of the Sovereign Lord is on me, because the Lord
> has anointed me to proclaim good news to the poor. He has
> sent me to bind up the brokenhearted, to proclaim freedom
> for the captives and release from darkness for the prisoners,
> to proclaim the year of the LORD's favor and the day of ven-
> geance of our God, to comfort all who mourn, and provide
> for those who grieve in Zion — to bestow on them a crown

---

[3] Paul Tautges, *Comfort the Grieving: Ministering God's Grace in Times of Loss* (Grand Rapids: Zondervan, 2014), 35.

of beauty instead of ashes, the oil of job instead of mourning, and a garment of praise instead of the spirit of despair. They will be called oaks of righteousness, a planting of the LORD for the display of his splendor."

Isa. 61:1-3, NIV

Howard Clinebell states, "Grief is involved in all significant changes, losses, and life transitions, not just in the death of a loved person."[4] In Judges 19 through 21, eleven tribes decided to let the tribe of Benjamin cease to exist. They were devastated by the decision and grieved the loss of fellowship.

After being released from Babylonian captivity, Israelites mourned their disobedience to God. Ezra 10:6 recounts, "Then Ezra withdrew from before the house of God and went to the room of Jehohanan son of Eliashib. While he was there, he ate no food and drank no water, because he continued to mourn over the unfaithfulness of the exiles."

Nehemiah got the news about Jerusalem and said, "When I heard these things, I sat down and wept. For some days I mourned and fasted and prayed before the God of heaven." (Neh. 1:4, NIV) He expressed his grief and chose to do what it took to change the conditions in Jerusalem. It is normal to search for the good and the purpose in suffering. Could troubles that

---

[4] Howard Clinebell, *Basic Types of Pastoral Care & Counseling: Resources for the Ministry of Healing and Growth* (Nashville: Abingdon, 1984), 219.

bring about suffering, grieving, and mourning be the means to personal transformation?

Job is an example of how life suddenly changed due to forces over which he had no control. R. Kelvin Moore provides two reasons to focus on Job for this study. He states, "A survey of the book of Job shows the universality of suffering and its extensiveness [that includes] pain, illness, and death [along with] experiences of profound hurt and loneliness."[5] Second, Moore says, "Job affirmed that life as it comes, along with joys, is beset by hurt, betrayal, loneliness, disease, threat, anxiety, bewilderment, anger, hatred, and anguish. All human beings suffer."[6] Grieving can help us develop strong character and confident hope as we get to experience the love of God in ways previously unknown to us. Grieving can be a means to becoming the person we were created to be.

> "We can rejoice, too, when we run into problems and trials, for we know that they help us develop endurance. And endurance develops strength of character, and character strengthens our confident hope of salvation. And this hope will not lead to disappointment. For we know how dearly God loves us, because he has given us the Holy Spirit to fill our hearts with his love."
>
> Rom. 5:3-5, NLT

The Stages of Change presented in Prochaska's book were the inspiration for the principles that make up the tool kit of skills. I applied them to Job's suffering. Through comparison and contrast, I developed a set of

---

[5] R. Kelvin Moore, *The Psalms of Lamentation and the Enigma of Suffering*, (Lewiston, NY: Mellen, 1996), 3.

[6] Ibid.

principles for a tool kit called *A Theory of Grief.* The six Stages of Change are pre-contemplation, contemplation, preparation, action, maintenance, and termination.

The apostle Paul says, "Don't copy the behavior and customs of this world, but let God transform you into a new person by changing the way you think. Then you will learn to know God's will for you, which is good and pleasing and perfect." (Rom. 12:2, NLT) *A Theory of Grief* will show how *crises, conflict, considerations,* and *confrontation* helped Job and his friends change the way they thought about trouble. Ultimately, they were *transformed* and came to know God's good, pleasing, and perfect will for them.

These principles do not describe a mental or emotional condition. They represent a means to accomplish a purpose or shape an outcome. This theory is like a tool kit rather than a state of being or stages in a process. When we apply the characteristics of each principle to portions of Scripture in the book of Job, we understand how the skills worked as he and his friends were being transformed. First, we will identify the crises presented in Job 1:1-2:8 and relate them to how Job expressed his grief. Second, we will observe conflicts that arose in Job 2:8-3:26 and witness Job's struggle to reconcile the differences between his physical and spiritual realities. The rest of our discussions are based on Job 4 to Job 42. Third, we will see how Job and his friends incorporate emotional, social, and spiritual concerns as they consider how to respond to Job's suffering. Fourth, we will become aware of the issues Job confronted and pay attention to how he reacted. Finally, we will summarize what we learned about grief and how it contributed to their personal transformation.

Prochaska suggests, "Matching your challenges to your stage of change will help maximize your problem-solving efforts."[7] Similarly, *A Theory of*

---

[7] Prochaska, *Changing for Good,* 39

Grief consists of skills that can help us learn to know God and allow suffering to bring about the transformation called for by the apostle Paul in his letter to the Romans. Grieving can help us cope with change and get to the other side of trouble. Responding to crises by recognizing conflicts between feelings and faith; considering and weighing benefits of consolation and information; and choosing to confront concerns that stand in the way of progress are useful skills. According to Moore, "[They help to] delineate reasons for, reactions to and resolutions for suffering."[8]

---

[8] Moore, *The Psalms of Lamentation*, 2

CHAPTER 2

Crises Matter

"Praise be to the God and Father of our Lord Jesus Christ, the Father of compassion and the God of all comfort, who comforts us in all our troubles, so that we can comfort those in any trouble with the comfort we ourselves receive from God." 2 Cor. 1:3-4, NIV

Crises

Crises can be critical agents of change. They come in many forms. Some describe them as trouble, trials, tribulations, or tests. We do not always choose, anticipate, or welcome change. In his book *The Psalms of Lamentation and the Enigma of Suffering*, R. Kelvin Moore said, "The term 'suffering' in its broadest definition [is used] to describe anything undesirable or unpleasant."[9] Moore says, "There is no doubt that one who suffers is feeling pain or distress. Crises are often the source of suffering. They include physical or personal tragedies, emotional upheavals, or the like along with turning points, for better or worse."[10]

---

[9] Moore, *The Psalms of Lamentation*, 2.

[10] Ibid.

Scripture is not silent on the extensive impact of loss. The Bible acknowledges and addresses a full range of reasons and sources of suffering. Warren Wiersbe says, "Job is not a fictional character invented for this dramatic poem; he is a real man in history. Ezekiel names him (14:14-20) and so does James (5:11)."[11] Believing Job was a real man and looking carefully at his suffering can help us relate to his predicament. The tragedies Job experienced were totally unexpected. Job represents us in so many ways. We can learn from how he coped with crises and apply those skills to our own lives.

In the first of six Stages of Change that Prochaska called pre-contemplation, "individuals do not intend to take action [to change] in the near future."[12] Pre-contemplation does not apply to the narratives between Satan and the Lord because Job was not part of the heavenly conversation.

There is no evidence in the first five verses of the first chapter of Job that he was planning to change anything. He appeared to be content with his life and his worship. His children had more than enough of everything they needed to enjoy life. "His sons used to hold feasts in their homes on their birthdays, and they would invite their three sisters to eat and drink with them." (Job 1:4, NIV) There is a footnote in the Amplified Bible for this verse that states, "The Hebrew wording indicates . . . that *his* refers to each of the brothers in turn and since there were seven of them, it follows that they held a banquet every day of the week, rotating from house to house, as is indicated in verse 5. This is evidence both of the brothers' prosperity and the close relationship they maintained with one another."

Even though there is no indication that their gatherings were ungodly, Job tried to keep his children from suffering consequences of their

---

[11] Warren W. Wiersbe, *Wiersbe's Expository Outline on the Old Testament*, (Colorado Springs: Cook, 1993), 410.

[12] James O. Prochaska and Janice M. Prochaska, *Changing to Thrive*, (Center City: Hazelden, 2016), 1.

potential misdeeds. He anticipated that seven days of celebrations were liable to result in some type of trouble. We are informed, "When a period of feasting had run its course, Job would make arrangements for them to be purified. Early in the morning he would sacrifice a burnt offering for each of them, thinking, 'Perhaps my children have sinned and cursed God in their hearts.' This was Job's regular custom." (Job 1:5, NIV)

Job had no idea that in spite of his commitment to keep himself and his family pure before God, his life was about to be changed by one crisis after another.

> "One day when Job's sons and daughters were feasting and drinking wine at the oldest brother's house, a messenger came to Job and said, 'The oxen were plowing and the donkeys were grazing nearby, and the Sabeans attacked and made off with them. They put the servants to the sword, and I am the only one who has escaped to tell you!'"
>
> Job 1:13-15, NIV

Job's children were engaged in their usual festivities. Suddenly, a celebration changed into a crisis. His adversaries stole his livestock and killed those who worked for him. Along with stealing his property, they immediately deprived him of the ability to produce food and plow his fields. Job's wealth was measured by how much livestock he owned and how many people worked for him. Job's life changed immediately upon hearing the first servant's report. Suddenly, he was confronted with the crises of death and destruction.

All of this happened at the home of one of Job's son. That messenger did not mention or report on the other children. "While he was still speaking, another messenger came and said, "The fire of God fell from the heavens and burned up the sheep and the servants, and I am the only one who has escaped to tell you!'" (Job 1:16, NIV) Job had to process reports of 2 trage-dies with only 2 survivors while he absorbed the news that he had no sheep and no shepherds. It appears that lightening caused the disaster which left Job's land covered with dead animals and dead people.

The amount of devastation is hard for us to comprehend and Job did not get a chance to take it in. "While he was still speaking, another mes-senger came and said, 'The Chaldeans formed three raiding parties and swept down on your camels and made off with them. They put the ser-vants to the sword, and I am the only one who has escaped to tell you!'" (Job 1:17, NIV) Three of his enemies came together to steal more of his livestock and more of his servants. The assaults had escalated. It seemed like very little remained. Job experienced an abnormal amount of loss in a short period of time.

> "While he was still speaking, yet another messenger came and
> said, 'Your sons and daughters were feasting and drinking
> wine at the oldest brother's house, when suddenly a mighty
> wind swept in from the desert and struck the four corners of
> the house. It collapsed on them and they are dead, and I am
> the only one who has escaped to tell you!'" (Job 1:18-19, NIV)

Finally, Job received the message parents dread. The loss of servants and shepherds could in no way compare to losing all of his children — seven sons and three daughters. As much as he loved them, they could no longer return his affection. As much as they enjoyed the stability of belonging to a closely connected and financially secure family, wind destroyed a house and an entire generation of their family. There would be no grandchildren to inherit and enjoy the fruits of Job's wealth. With no sons, Job and his wife would likely be pitied rather than esteemed.

We will refer to Maslow's Hierarchy of Human Needs to help us understand the impact such extensive losses could have on Job. A. H. Maslow says, "Loss can be described as the inability to maintain or retain what you had.[13] With the death of his children, Job was deprived of heirs. He would not enjoy the love, belonging, and intimacy of extended family relationships. Job's servants had their sense of safety and security stolen when enemies took all the livestock. Job lost his reputation as the richest person in the area. Onlookers may conclude that Job had lost the Lord's favor. In spite of everything he experienced, Job mourned by worshipping the Lord instead of cursing.

Job's outpouring of grief was normal but his response to the avalanche of horrible crises announced by each messenger may have been unexpected. Job was not part of the heavenly conversation between Satan and the Lord. Without his knowledge, Job had been enlisted in a spiritual war that was going to be fought in the earthly realm. Whether he was ready or not, the battles had already begun. Satan was counting on him to curse the Lord. Try to imagine how disappointed Satan must have been when he saw a bald headed man in ragged clothes praising the Lord. In other words, Job chose to humbly bless the Lord at *that* time just as he had done all the time before.

Job was not given an opportunity for pre-contemplation or contemplation. He had no time to prepare for change or to even be persuaded to change. He was forced to cope with the immediate crises that overtook him. He had to deal with relentless, extreme emergencies. Some happened by accident and some were intentional. His enemies lived close enough that he may have anticipated that someday they were liable to

---

[13] A. H. Maslow, *A Theory of Human Motivation* (Connecticut: Martino Publishing, 2013), 14.

attack him. Yes, death is inevitable. Job had no idea that death was imminent for his children.

Job's reality changed in a very short period of time. All of Job's children died — seven sons and three daughters. All but one of Job's farmhands died. All but one of Job's shepherds died. All but four of Job's servants died and all of Job's oxen, donkeys, and camels were stolen. Lightning struck and burned up all of his sheep. A strong wind caused the oldest brother's house to collapse. I group crises in six categories — death, disease, disability, deficiency, decisions, and destruction. The record shows that Job experienced death, deficiency, and destruction in Satan's first visit.

> "Job stood up and tore his robe in grief. Then he shaved his head and fell to the ground to worship. He said, 'I came naked from my mother's womb, and I will be naked when I leave. The LORD gave me what I had, and the LORD has taken it away. Praise the name of the LORD!' In all of this, Job did not sin by blaming God."
>
> Job 1:20-22, NLT

Job prioritized worship over robes. He prioritized worship over hair. He prioritized worship over wonder. Job decided to praise the name of the Lord. He acknowledged that God retained the rights of ownership for everything and everybody in creation. Job already knew the truth of what the apostle Paul wrote in his first letter to the church at Thessalonica. "Give thanks in all circumstances; for this is God's will for you in Christ Jesus." (1 Thess. 5:18, NIV)

Even though Job's grieving began with worship, his response should not be interpreted as the only acceptable or permissible reaction. Every person has their own way of mourning. In Hebrews 4:15 the writer lets us know that Jesus empathizes with us and understands how we feel. One tragedy after another caused a change in the reason Job worshipped. He used to worship, sacrifice, and praise the Lord *just in case* he or his family had sinned. Now Job was *provoked* to worship and crises left no time for contemplation or pre-contemplation. Job worshipped and praised the Lord to help him cope with the relentless onslaught of crises. Even though trouble changed the purpose of his worship from prevention to conviction, Job maintained unshakeable faith in the Lord.

Blessing the Lord instead of blaming him did not make Job trouble-proof. His faith was tested and perseverance still had work to do in him. Peter's warning could have helped Job. He said, "Stay alert! Watch out for your great enemy, the devil. He prowls around like a roaring lion, looking for someone to devour." (1 Pet. 5:8, NLT) That was exactly what was about to happen to Job and there was no way he could avoid taking his next test.

"So Satan went out from the presence of the LORD and afflicted Job with painful sores from the soles of his feet to the crown of his head." (Job 2:7, NIV) Job's trouble moved up to the next level. Job had to deal with another crisis that had a more devastating effect. He had a disease with an unknown prognosis. He had no idea how long he would have to live in that state of health.

Job's condition created a crisis for his wife. He could have been the only immediate family she had left. She lost her children, livestock, servants, and status also. Who would share her grief? Who would comfort and console her? She lost the companionship of her husband due to a disease that required him to be in isolation. She expressed her feelings when she encouraged Job to give up. "His wife said to him, 'Are you still maintaining your integrity? Curse God and die!'" (Job 2:9, NIV) Job was not moved nor did he sin.

Like Job, we face troubles that are hard to understand. There is consolation and comfort in God's Word. The prophet Jeremiah poured out his heart to the Lord in the book of Lamentations. In his letter to the Corinthian church, Paul talked about being patient in difficult times. He listed some of the crises he had endured in 2 Corinthians 6:4-5. Jesus said that he was giving peace to his followers as a replacement for trouble or fear in John 14:27. Suffering can be the cause or result of relational or spiritual instability. In John 13:21 Jesus was troubled in his spirit. Jesus understood that our hearts can be troubled. That is why He said, "Do not let your hearts be troubled. You believe in God; believe also in me." (John 14:1, NIV) Jesus acknowledged in John 12:27 that His soul was troubled when he talked about His death. In some biblical versions or translations, trials and tribulations are described as suffering. Jesus said, "I have told you all this so that you may have peace in me. Here on earth you will have many trials and sorrows. But take heart, because I have overcome the world." (Jn. 16:33, NLT) Job relied on his resolute faith in God to sustain him.

CHAPTER 3

Conflict Matters

"My dear brothers and sisters, take note of this: Everyone should be quick to listen, slow to speak and slow to become angry," James 1:19, NIV

Many who experienced suffering would like to have known in advance what the Lord was trying to accomplish in them. Conflict arises when reasoning does not follow logic. There is nothing in the Stages of Change model that compares to that type of emotional imbalance. Conflict describes Job's struggle to reconcile his unwavering faith in God with how he felt and the facts of his condition.

His grief is on full display in chapter three. Job's body, mind, and spirit were in disharmony. Varunaj Churnai explains, "[Conflict can result from the] struggle, emotional disturbance, clash, or contradictions [that exist between physical and spiritual realities.][14] She goes on to say, "Job's friends

---

[14] Varunaj Churnai, *Beyond Justice: Death and the Retribution Principle in the Book of Job* (Carlisle, UK: Langham Monographs, 2018), loc. 1480, Kindle.

maintained that the righteous are rewarded and the wicked are punished by a righteous God in this earthly life."[15]

Job's suffering problem clashed with human reasoning. There seemed to be irreconcilable differences between the life Job expected to maintain and the changes being forced upon him. We find that even the psalmist supported this position when he penned, "Blessed is the one who does not walk in step with the wicked or stand in the way that sinners take or sit in the company of mockers, but whose delight is in the law of the Lord, and who meditates on his law day and night." (Ps.1:1-2, NIV)

Job had an emotional and spiritual response to hearing from the messengers about the loved ones, servants, and property he lost. Job followed up ripping his robe and cutting his hair with worshipping and praising the Lord. Instead of conflict between his feelings and his faith, they were able to mutually coexist. His reality put pressure on his faith but he did not yield to any impulse that could tempt him to dishonor God.

Job prayed and sacrificed for himself and his household to prevent tragedies and position his family to be blessed. He easily fit the description of a godly man. He distinguished himself from the ungodly. Godly men prosper. They do not lose everything. Except for his wife and a few servants, all that Job owned had been blown away. He did the right things and the wrong things happened to him. In spite of everything he went through, Job honored and obeyed the Lord. Someone in his situation might wonder how much more it would take to avoid hurt and achieve happiness.

Churnai says, "There is tension between death [loss] as divine judgement and death as a gateway to eternal life with God."[16] Death, destruction, and disease were inconsistent with the blessings associated with faithfulness to God, consistent worship, and upright living. We see how Job dealt

---

[15] Ibid.

[16] Churnai, *Beyond Justice*, loc. 542.

with inconsistencies in 4 passages. First, Job lost his wealth during the events reported in Job 1:8-17. Second, he lost his children in Job 1:18-19. Third, Job lost his health in Job 2:7-10. Finally, in Job 3:1-26 we get to look through the window into Job's struggle with the prospect of being seriously ill for the rest of his life. Job lost his peace.

Job and his wife did not agree on the solution to his problems. They had to cope with death and disaster along with a dis-abling, destructive disease that deprived him of health, well-ness, love, intimacy, self-esteem, and acceptance. Scripture does not  examine the impact of Job's crises on his wife. However, I want to take this opportunity to discuss some of the ways trouble, trials, and tests affect the lives of others.

Please allow me this point of personal privilege. By reading into the text some consideration for Job's wife, I will examine how she shared in his suffering. His crises and losses became her crises and losses. She was a witness to and a participant in much of what he went through.

His trouble changed her life. *Their* children were dead. *Their* servants were dead. *Their* property was destroyed and *their* livestock was stolen. Because Job was so sick, *they* could anticipate the inevitable sting of death. Attitudes often change when death appears imminent. Job and his wife had no idea where they were on life's journey. Job could have survived for a long time in his debilitated condition. Even though he had other family and friends, he was required to live in isolation. His wife and their remaining servants could have been his only caregivers.

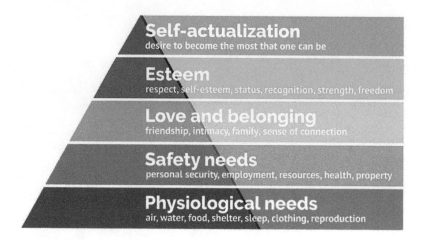

Maslow's hierarchy of needs

Maslow's Hierarchy of Human Needs throws light onto the possible effects of his condition on her future. She lost the esteem of being wealthy. She would be deprived of his good health and sexual intimacy. She may have agreed when Job expressed his feelings by saying, "My breath is repulsive to my wife; I am loathsome to my own family." (Job 19:17, NIV).

Grief care for her husband could have been enmeshed with grief care for herself. She realized that Job was the only one who could solve their problem. "His wife said to him, 'Are you still trying to maintain your integrity? Curse God and die!'" (Job 2:9, NIV) Unlike a fool who says there is no God, his wife seemed to suggest that Job misplaced his faith in God. Was she expressing more confidence in Job's integrity than in God's faithfulness?

His wife's feelings appeared to be in conflict with Job's faith. In Deuteronomy 32:28, Moses described the Israelites as senseless and foolish because they were without understanding. It has been said, "Spouting off before listening to the facts is both shameful and foolish." (Prov. 18:13,

NLT) Additionally, "Those who trust their own insight are foolish, but anyone who walks in wisdom is safe." (Prov. 28:26, NLT) Fortunately, Job recognized foolishness in his wife and resisted the urge to please her. "He replied, 'You are talking like a foolish woman. Shall we accept good from God, and not trouble?' In all this, Job did not sin in what he said." (Job 2:10, NIV) He could answer her question with a question because, for him, the answer was obvious. Job 31:9-10 helps us understand Job when he said, "If my heart has been seduced by a woman, or if I have lusted for my neighbor's wife, then let my wife serve another man; let other men sleep with her." He was so sure that he had nothing for which to repent that he was willing to submit to the ultimate disrespect of having his wife become intimate with another man.

Her question could have been a cry for help. She asked him a question that she may have already asked herself. Their present situation was not what the Lord promised those who worshipped him and lived according to his commands. She could have been expressing anger, frustration, exasperation, or resentment. She could have been sad or disappointed, ashamed, discouraged, or disconsolate. Those emotions and more are natural and normal responses to loss. In any case, Job did not acknowledge her feelings. He quickly defended his faith in God and dismissed her question by calling her foolish.

I created this scenario to bring attention to how important it is that we empathize with Job's wife and others like her. No one's grief should be overlooked or minimized. It is not unusual for mourners to blame God for their pain. Her cry was answered with criticism instead of compassion. Because everyone with a broken heart matters, we want to be sensitive and take every opportunity to comfort, console, and bless those who mourn.

Family and friends tend to be reliable first responders in times of trouble. "When three of Job's friends heard of the tragedy he had suffered, they got together and traveled from their homes to comfort and console him. Their names were Eliphaz the Temanite, Bildad the Shuhite, and Zophar the Naamathite." (Job 2:11, NLT) Job's friends left home on assignment to share Job's grief. Their reaction to seeing Job at a distance was an indication of how the disease had ravaged his body. They wept, expressed their grief, shared his ashes, and sat with Job in silence for seven days and nights. They were so overwhelmed with compassion that words failed them. Sometimes presence is effective ministry and satisfies the greatest need.

Varunaj Churnai explains how conflict can be a natural outcome in certain situations. Regarding Job's friends, she says, "They maintained that the righteous are rewarded and the wicked are punished by a righteous God in this earthly life."[17] After they regained their ability to speak, Job would have to defend himself against their insistence that sin was at the root of his suffering. He resisted the temptation to entertain the idea that God was being unjust. He was steadfast in the fight for his faith with his wife and his friends. He also had to deal with the conflict within.

Job broke the seven-day silence by venting his frustration with his situation. His body and spirit were disturbed. Job's grief was on full display in Job 3:1-10. He concluded that he would not be in trouble now had he never been born. Instead of cursing God, he cursed the day he was born. His lament covered conception, childbirth, life, and suffering. He reasoned that death was a way out of his misery and he seemed to welcome it. Grief can complicate managing the inclination to blame God without defaming God.

Job redefined joy and sorrow by inverting birth and death. According to Job 3:11-15, he envisioned himself at peace in a place with princes if he had been allowed to die instead of being born. Without cursing God, Job challenged God's decision to bring him to life. His grief was so great that he concluded death should come sooner rather than later.

---

[17] Ibid.

Job moved back and forth between emotional collapse and spiritual uplift in Job 3:20-26. He asked thought provoking questions throughout chapter three. His opening statement was his conclusion: the way to avoid dying is to not have existed. Though true, that observation was not helpful in his current state. Job did not give in to his feelings. He kept talking to his friends. For more than 30 chapters, we find Job considering his friend's spiritual explanations for his earthly condition. "A friend loves at all times, and a brother is born for a time of adversity." (Prov. 17:17, NIV) It will become evident how Job benefited from saying what was in his heart and having someone to hear what was on his mind.

CHAPTER 4

Consideration Matters

"I meditate on your precepts and consider your ways." Ps. 119:15, NIV

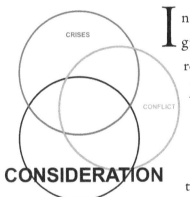

I n *Beyond Justice*, Varunaj Churnai describes grief caregivers and affirms their role and responsibility. She states, "The mission of Job's three friends [was] 'to console and comfort Job,' the greatest man of the east" (2:11; cf 1:3).[18] They left their homes and traveled great distances to share in his suffering. As they approached him, the men were so overwhelmed by his appearance that they joined him in what Churnai describes "the kind of 'ritual' [that] signified that they [had] come not only to encourage Job to move on with his life but also to acknowledge a journey that [could hasten his] death."[19] Consideration is the principle similar to contemplation from the Stages of Change.

Prochaska states, "Contemplators struggle to understand their problems, see its causes, and to wonder about possible solutions."[20] Job's

---

[18] Churnai, *Beyond Justice*, loc. 1505.

[19] Ibid., loc. 1518.

[20] Prochaska, *Changing for Good*, 42.

attitude seemed to match the description of one in the contemplation Stage of Change, but there is a significant difference. Contemplators tend to focus on solutions. Those employing consideration focus on the cause. Contemplators are often dealing with prior failures in their attempts to change. Job was seeking an explanation for his situation and he pondered the merits of each suggestion. He was desperate to understand why he was unprotected from troubles, trials, tests, and the changes they brought.

Job's conversation with his friends went beyond gathering information to weighing the emotional, social, and spiritual factors that could have adversely affected his life. Job and his friends were asking and trying to answer typical questions under the circumstances. In *Caring for People God's Way*, Clinton explains that the grieved are often obsessed with meta-questions such as, "Why? How could *you* let this happen, God? Why me?"[21] What could Job have done to prevent this? How should Job explain to others what has happened to him?

Churnai reveals in *Beyond Justice* that Job and his friends based their understanding of the Lord's Justice on the common practice known as retribution. She says, "*Retribution* [is] the popular theology according to which the righteous prosper but the wicked suffer."[22] Most of the conversation between Job and his friends centered on whether Job was innocent. In the presence of such extreme suffering, Eliphaz, Bildad, Zophar, and Elihu staked out positions that justified their thoughts about God by viewing Job's situation through the lens of their experiences.

Compassionate grief caregivers consider ways to alleviate suffering and relieve pain. Job's friends were less interested in relieving his suffering than

---

[21] Tim Clinton, Archibald Hart, and George Ohlschlager, eds., *Caring for People God's Way: Personal and Emotional Issues, Addictions, Grief, and Trauma* (Nashville: Thomas Nelson, Inc., 2006), 365.

[22] Craig S. Keener and John H. Walton, *NIV Cultural Backgrounds Study Bible*, (Grand Rapids: Zondervan, 2016).

they were in pinpointing his failure. These men engaged in marathon sessions to persuade Job to do what it would take to turn things around. They asserted, "If only you would prepare your heart and lift up your hands to him in prayer! Get rid of your sins, and leave all iniquity behind you. Your life will be brighter than the noonday. Even darkness will be as bright as morning." (Job 11:13-14, 17, NLT) After seven days of silence, their conversations

seemed to contribute to Job's upheaval because they insisted on sharing what they thought they knew about God's plan for Job's suffering.

With their input, Job formed judgments and came to his own conclusions about the condition of his relationship with the Lord. He finally responded, "Have mercy on me, my friends, have mercy, for the hand of God has struck me. Must you also persecute me, like God does? Haven't you chewed me up enough?" (Job 19:21-22, NLT) Even though he refused to plead guilty to any offense, the debate provided a forum for Job to affirm his faith in God's character. That discussion set the stage for a transformative encounter with God.

Job was desperate to know why he was suffering so much. It mattered to him how his family and friends reacted to his trouble. He considered their explanations and carefully weighed them for relevance, strengths, weaknesses, and limitations. He implored his friend, Eliphaz, "Teach me, and I will keep quiet. Show me what I have done wrong." (Job 6:24, NLT) Job did not ask to be delivered. He wanted to know and understand *why* he was in such misery. Churnai said,

"They work the logic of this theory backward: suffering is a sign of wrongdoing on the part of the sufferer; prosperity is a sign of virtuous action. Job suffers; therefore he has sinned. Given their perspective, death is understood to be the ultimate recompense for sin. Significantly, in their retributive worldview, it is not a natural death, but a terrified death Job is experiencing that represents the ultimate recompense from God (e.g. 4:9; 8:3-6; 11:20)"[23]

Grievers often want to know if good will come from suffering. Churnai acknowledged that sufferers search for comforting solutions to their problems. "The retribution principle as a theme [was] explicitly generated from the friends, not from Job."[24] She goes on to say,

"In analyzing Job's understanding of death ... Job, in effect, also has two faces: he is alternately defiant and faithful. Sometimes it is the struggling or defiant Job who speaks of death as the dismal termination of life (e.g. 10:18-22). At other times the faithful Job struggles to look beyond physical death and has hope in [the Lord]. (e.g. 14:14; 16:18-21; 17:6-16; 19:25-27)[25]

Job praised the Lord by saying, "For God is so wise and so mighty. Who has ever challenged him successfully? He does great things too marvelous to understand. He performs countless miracles." (Job 9:4, 10, NLT) He was not satisfied with his friends' advice. Job declared, "Wisdom belongs

---

[23] Churnai, *Beyond Justice*, loc. 1480.

[24] Ibid.

[25] Ibid., loc. 1493.

to the aged, and understanding to the old. 'But true wisdom and power are found in God; counsel and understanding are his.'" (Job 12:12-13, NLT) With clarity, Job made it known that he may have been confused about the basis of God's decisions, but he had no doubt they were wise.

If Job's friends understood retribution to be punishment or reward in this life based entirely on performance in this life, then Job's suffering was consistent with a just God. They reasoned that Job's circumstances must have been payment for his sins. Did justice require numerous crises of this magnitude? William Mounce declares, "In the Old Testament justice or judgment carries a legal or judicial connotation, though it is used in a variety of ways. It is often used in the context of some sort of dispute, whether between two differing human parties or between God and Israel."[26]

Job seemed to be getting the silent treatment in a dispute with the Lord and he was desperate to settle it. Maybe he had displeased the Lord in some way, but he did not remember committing the offense. Mounce says, "This theme of the absolute *justice* of God is an important one in the book of Job, where one of Job's main arguments against his 'friends' is that God cannot pervert justice (Job 8:3; 9:19). God confirms this sentiment at the end of the book when he states that *justice* is one of his chief characteristics (40:8).[27]

Even so, Job may have shared the sentiment of the psalmist who said, "Did I keep my heart pure for nothing? Did I keep myself innocent for no reason? I get nothing but trouble all day long; every morning brings me pain." (Ps 73:13-14, NLT) As Job progressed through his grieving, most of the conversation between Job and his friends included periods of reasoning during which they considered all possible logical explanations for

---

[26] William D. Mounce, ed., *Mounce's Complete Expository Dictionary of Old and New Testament Words* (Grand Rapids: Zondervan, 2006), 373.

[27] Ibid.

Job's situation. While Job was willing to examine his life, Job was convinced he was being mistreated. His friends often projected their attitudes onto God. Churnai recognizes,

> "The traditional theory of retribution is reflected in the book of Proverbs. . . . The theory is biblical, namely there is a connection between sin and suffering: prosperity is attained by the wise and virtuous, but destruction is the fate of the foolish and wicked. Significantly, the blessing or punishment is attributed to the direct intervention of God. But 'the book of Job is a vehement attack on this view.[28]

Job was in constant conflict with his friends. Churnai maintains, "During the disputations with the friends, Job repeatedly requested a trial with God, so that he might directly present his case as an innocent sufferer, and eventually hear from God himself the charges which might be laid against him and thus be able to refute them (9:3,14-20,28-35; 13:22,23; 23:3-17; 31:35-37)."[29]

Each of Job's friends spoke what they knew about the Lord as if it were all there was to be known about Him. What did Job and his friends think they knew about God? Eliphaz believed he was seeing God discipline the one who disobeyed him. He seemed to equate suffering with punishment. He suggested that Job missed the mark in some way. In Job 5:24, Eliphaz assured Job that he would remember sinning and failing to repent if he thought long and hard enough.

Eliphaz was confident in the Lord's justice. With so many losses, Eliphaz implied that it was obvious Job was guilty of something when he

---

[28] Churnai, *Beyond Justice*, loc. 498.

[29] Churnai, *Beyond Justice*, loc. 3437.

said, "From six calamities he will rescue you; in seven no harm will touch you." (Job 5:19, NIV) Eliphaz asserted his expertise when he disclosed, "We have studied life and found all this to be true. Listen to my counsel, and apply it to yourself." (Job 5:27, NLT) Later, he urged Job to listen to himself saying, "Your own mouth condemns you, not I. Your own lips testify against you." (Job 15:6, NLT) Eliphaz asked, "Were you listening at God's secret council? Do you have a monopoly on wisdom?" (Job 15:8, NLT) Eliphaz expressed his conviction when he said, "The wicked writhe in pain throughout their lives. Years of trouble are stored up for the ruthless." (Job 15:20, NLT) The evidence spoke for itself. Job appeared to be getting his just reward.

Eliphaz reasoned that Job and God were not operating in the same physical, emotional, or spiritual realm. He explained, "God is so great – higher than the heavens, higher than the farthest stars. But you reply, 'That's why God can't see what I'm doing! How can he judge through the thick darkness? For thick clouds swirl about him, and he cannot see us. He is way up there, walking on the vault of heaven.'" (Job 22:12-14, NLT) Eliphaz advised Job that he could control his situation by making peace with God. In Job 22:21-23, Eliphaz offers his explanation of the relationship between prosperity and wickedness. Maybe Job and God were misunderstanding each other and they needed to bridge the gulf between them.

Bildad asked, "Does God pervert justice? Does the Almighty pervert what is right?" (Job 8:3, NIV) He goes on to answer those questions by considering all that happened to Job. He suggested in Job 8:4 that Job's suffering was proof that he and his family sinned. Maybe Job could manage these hard times by applying what he learned from his elders. They might have said, "But if you will seek God earnestly and plead with the Almighty, if you are pure and upright, even now he will rouse himself on your behalf and restore you to your prosperous state. Your beginnings will seem humble, so prosperous will your future be." (Job 8:5-7, NIV)

Bildad believed, "The lamp of a wicked man is snuffed out; the flame of his fire stops burning." (Job 18:5, NIV) In other words, bad things only happen to the corrupt. Bildad claimed to know God much better than Job. It is as if he was trying to get Job to accept his fate as a sinner when he said,

> "Fire resides in his tent; burning sulfur is scattered over his
> dwelling. His roots dry up below and branches wither above.
> The memory of him perishes from the earth; he has no name
> in the land. He is driven from light into the realm of dark-
> ness and is banished from the world. He has no offspring or
> descendants among his people, no survivor where once he
> lived. People of the west are appalled at his fate; those of the
> east are seized with horror. Surely such is the dwelling of an
> evil man; such is the place of one who does not know God."
> Job 18:15-21, NIV

Zophar believed that God knew what Job did and he wished God would speak up and tell everybody. In Job 11:5-6 Zophar suggests that he knows God has forgotten some of Job's sin. He concedes that God's ways are mysterious and without limits. Therefore, who knows why God does what he does? Zophar pointed out, "Surely he recognizes deceivers; and when he sees evil, does he not take note? If you put away the sin that is in your hand and allow no evil to dwell in your tent, then, free of fault, you will lift up your face; you will stand firm and without fear." (Job 11:11, 14-15, NIV) After further discussion, Zophar recounted historical prece-dence and stated, "Surely you know how it has been from of old, ever since mankind was placed on the earth, that the mirth of the wicked is brief, the joy of the godless lasts but a moment." (Job 20:4-5, NIV)

After Eliphaz, Bildad, and Zophar presented their circumstantial evidence, Elihu seemed to abandon the original mission of comfort and compassion. We learn, "But Elihu son of Barakel the Buzite, of the family of Ram, became very angry with Job for justifying himself rather than God. He was also angry with the three friends, because they had found no way to refute Job, and yet had condemned him." (Job 32:2-3, NIV) We have no idea how much time had passed, but no one appeared to move from their original positions. Job was relentless and Elihu showed respect for his elders by letting them speak before him.

The three friends declared what they believed they knew about the Lord and how He related to those who were faithful and obedient. The old men kept asking Job for answers but refused to listen. It was finally time to hear what a wise young man knew about the Lord and His ways. Elihu said, "I gave you my full attention. But none of you has proved Job wrong; none of you has answered his arguments. Do not say, 'We have found wisdom; let God, not a man, refute him.'" (Job 32:12-13, NIV)

Elihu goes on to give examples of how the Lord preserves and protects his people. He concluded that the Lord spares his people from danger even when he chastens them. Elihu shared his personal experience when he said,

> "For God does speak – now one way, now another – though no one perceives it. In a dream, in a vision of the night, when deep sleep falls on people as they slumber in their beds, he may speak in their ears and terrify them with warnings, to turn them from wrongdoing and keep them from pride, to preserve them from the pit, their lives from perishing by the sword. Or someone may be chastened on a bed of pain

with constant distress in their bones, so that their body finds food repulsive and their soul loathes the choicest meal. Their flesh wastes away to nothing, and their bones, once hidden, now stick out. They draw near to the pit, and their life to the messengers of death. Yet if there is an angel at their side, a messenger, one out of a thousand, sent to tell them how to be upright, and he is gracious to that person and says to God, 'Spare them from going down to the pit; I have found a ransom for them – let their flesh be renewed like a child's; let them be restored as in the days of their youth' – then that person can pray to God and find favor with him, they will see God's face and shout for joy; he will restore them to full well-being." (Job 33:14-26, NIV)

Tom Milazzo explains, "For the righteous . . . suffering and death would be bearable if only God's reason for subjecting them to their agony were known. Yet it seems that even when revealed, that reason remains incomprehensible."[30] He goes on to say, "So long as God is silent, we do not know whether we suffer by the hand of God or by God's absence."[31] Job and his friends continued to struggle because there simply had to be answers to their questions. Milazzo seems to encourage persistence when he says,

"The promise of wisdom, however, is that the ways of God will be opened, unveiled to human beings, so that we might understand and grasp all that is hidden from us. Implicitly, the promise of wisdom is that in grasping the ways of God,

---

[30] Tom G. Milazzo, *The Protest and the Silence: Suffering, Death, and Biblical Theology* (Minneapolis: Fortress Press, 1992), 43.

[31] Ibid., 45.

in seeing the order that underlies human existence and the world, the presence of God will itself emerge from the darkness. Understanding is the prelude to knowledge, which is the threshold of revelation. Revelation opens the darkness that enshrouds God and obscures its face from human being. Where there is darkness and mystery, wisdom seeks to offer certainty and knowledge. Where there was hiddenness, wisdom seeks to offer presence. Where there was the possibility that we suffer and die by the hand of God, wisdom seeks to proclaim God's innocence."[32]

Sometimes people need to be reassured. The prophet Isaiah said, "Although the Lord gives you the bread of adversity and the water of affliction, your teachers will be hidden no more; with your own eyes you will see them." (Isa. 30:20, NIV) Those who lived during New Testament times saw God in the flesh. Those living in the Old Testament could only see God through his mighty acts. Adversity provided an opportunity to see God in new ways and know him more intimately. According to the Latin saying by Benjamin Franklin as recorded in (*Poor Richard's Almanac*, Nov.1973), "Experience keeps a dear school, yet fools learn no other way."[33] In other words, we learn the most from some lessons because experience teaches them best.

Eliphaz reasoned, "Blessed is the one whom God corrects; so do not despise the discipline of the Almighty. For he wounds, but he also binds up; he injures, but his hands also heal." (Job 5:17-18, NIV) After asking

---

[32] Ibid.,121.

[33] Answers.com, accessed January 2, 2019, http://www.answers.com/Q/ Who said experience is the best teacher.

numerous questions, Eliphaz declared, "We have examined this, and it is true. So hear it and apply it to yourself." (Job 5:27, NIV)

Job continued discussing his situation with Bildad and Zophar. Eliphaz joined the conversation by saying, "Listen to me and I will explain to you; let me tell you what I have seen." (Job 15:17, NIV) Based on his experience, Eliphaz attested, "All his days the wicked man suffers torment, the ruthless man through all the years stored up for him. Terrifying sounds fill his ears; when all seems well, marauders attack him." (Job 15:20-21, NIV) He seemed to sympathize with Job's desperation to understand when he added, "Distress and anguish fill him with terror; troubles overwhelm him, like a king poised to attack, because he shakes his fist at God and vaunts himself against the Almighty, defiantly charging against him with a thick, strong shield." (Job 15:24-26, NIV)

Retribution has its limits. Job and his friends had a problem with the purpose of such a principle. Their despair continued to grow as they sought an explanation for Job's suffering. Based on their knowledge and understanding of God's reward system for blessing and cursing, they concluded the retribution system was working properly. Eliphaz understood trouble to be associated with God's anger and used the fundamentals of reaping what you sow to explain Job's predicament. Moore writes that Sheila Carney determined, "There is no Biblical foundation for the conception of an emotionless God worshipped by emotionless people. Carney insists that expressing anger to, or even at, Yahweh becomes an affirmation of God's existence and of our need to worship him."[34]

J. William Worden writes that [Kübler-Ross] states, "Anger is frequently experienced after a loss. It can be one of the most confusing feelings for the survivor and as such is at the root of many problems in the

---

[34] Moore, *Psalms of Lamentations*, 52.

grieving process."[35] Job seemed to agree with that analysis when he insisted, "Consider now: Who, being innocent, has ever perished? Where were the upright ever destroyed? As I have observed, those who plow evil and those who sow trouble reap it. At the breath of God they perish; at the blast of his anger they are no more." (Job 4:7-9, NIV)

Eliphaz sensed that Job could be harboring resentment because of what happened to his children. He suggested that Job should not expect that God would hear and answer his calls for help. Eliphaz maintained, "Resentment kills a fool, and envy slays the simple. I myself have seen a fool taking root, but suddenly his house was cursed. His children are far from safety, crushed in court without a defender." (Job 5:2-4, NIV) Was Eliphaz trying to prepare Job just in case God disappointed him?

Job answered Eliphaz by acknowledging man's helplessness when God exercises his powers. Job shared his opinion with Bildad when he said,

> "If he snatches away, who can stop him? Who can say to him,
> 'What are you doing?' God does not restrain his anger; even
> the cohorts of Rahab cowered at his feet. "How then can I
> dispute with him? How can I find words to argue with him?
> Though I were innocent, I could not answer him; I could only
> plead with my Judge for mercy."
>
> Job 9:12-15, NIV

Job explained that being innocent does not excuse one from trouble. With God being just in all his dealings and unrestricted, Job realized there was nothing he could say that would prove the injustice of his present state. Job admitted that he did not know whether there was a mysterious

---

[35] J. William Worden, *Grief Counseling and Grief Therapy: A Handbook for the Mental Health Practitioner.* 4th ed. (New York: Springer Publishing Company, 2009), 19.

connection between trouble and God's anger. Job's only explanation was a retribution checklist of possible explanations for suffering. Job just needed to know why these things happened to him and how to avoid their being repeated. Job also pointed to the relentlessness of his suffering. It was as if God's anger could only be satisfied when his body was covered with painful sores. Job shared with Bildad what he planned to tell God about how he felt. He lamented,

> "You gave me life and showed me kindness, and in your prov-
> idence watched over my spirit. "But this is what you con-
> cealed in your heart, and I know that this was in your mind:
> If I sinned, you would be watching me and would not let my
> offense go unpunished. If I am guilty—woe to me! Even if I
> am innocent, I cannot lift my head, for I am full of shame and
> drowned in my affliction. If I hold my head high, you stalk
> me like a lion and again display your awesome power against
> me. You bring new witnesses against me and increase your
> anger toward me; your forces come against me wave upon
> wave. "Why then did you bring me out of the womb? I wish
> I had died before any eye saw me. If only I had never come
> into being, or had been carried straight from the womb to
> the grave! Are not my few days almost over? Turn away from
> me so I can have a moment's joy before I go to the place of no
> return, to the land of gloom and utter darkness, to the land
> of deepest night, of utter darkness and disorder, where even
> the light is like darkness."
>
> Job 10:12-22, NIV

Now, Job seems to agree with Zophar that his misery could be attributed to God's anger. He mentions Sheol as a hiding place but does not associate Satan with his situation. He characterized God as having a type of temper tantrum that he would eventually get over. Job implored, "If only you would hide me in the grave and conceal me till your anger has passed! If only you would set me a time and then remember me! If someone dies, will they live again? All the days of my hard service I will wait for my renewal to come." (Job 14:13-14, NIV)

Eliphaz did not welcome Job's anger. He never heard his forefathers dare to publicly vent their anger. Job should have just quietly accepted his punishment and waited to see how God would conclude the matter. In other words, Job had a lot of nerve being angry with God. Instead of sympathy, Eliphaz denied Job permission to mourn when he said,

> "What do you know that we do not know? What insights do
> you have that we do not have? The gray-haired and the aged
> are on our side, men even older than your father. Are God's
> consolations not enough for you, words spoken gently to you?
> Why has your heart carried you away, and why do your eyes
> flash, so that you vent your rage against God and pour out
> such words from your mouth?"
>
> Job 15:9-13, NIV

In spite of what his friends preached, it was normal for Job to respond with angry outbursts. He was a spiritual, physical, and emotional being. He showed that grief, pain, and faith are not mutually exclusive. Faithful mourners should not be expected to suppress the pain of suffering and exhibit a constant state of joy. Churnai claimed, "God's desire is to deal mercifully and lovingly with people. However, when people violate God's holiness and justice, God will punish them with intent to bring sinner to repentance. On the other hand, if the sinner does not repent, his rejection will lead him to the ultimate recompense – death (e.g. Job 36:8-12)."[36]

Through the prophet Isaiah God declared, "I make known the end from the beginning, from ancient times, what is still to come. I say, 'My purpose will stand, and I will do all that I please.'" (Isa. 46:10) The psalmist assured, "He guides the humble in what is right and teaches them his way." (Ps. 25:9, NIV) Today, grief caregivers can be guided by the words of the apostle Paul when he said, "So we have stopped evaluating others from a human point of view. At one time we thought of Christ merely from a human point of view. How differently we know him now!" (2 Cor. 5:16, NLT)

Job and his friends teach us that what we have learned about God at any point in our lives is not all there is to be known. It really matters that we are able to consider what others say about God and receive their comfort as we grieve in our own way.

It is no accident that *Sovereign Lord* appeared at least 290 times in the New International Version of the Old Testament. When we study each occurrence, like Elihu, we might be reminded, "Look, God is all-powerful. Who is a teacher like him? No one can tell him what to do, or say to him, 'You have done wrong.'" (Job 36:22-23, NLT)

---

[36] Churnai, *Beyond Justice*, loc. 1505.

CHAPTER 5

Confrontation Matters

"I am not afraid of ten thousand enemies who surround me on every side.
Victory comes from you, O Lord. May you bless your people."
Ps. 3:6,8, NLT

Confrontation involves facing a problem and getting control by taking actions that may have positive or negative consequences. Stages of Change called preparation and action are combined in *A Theory of Grieving* to describe confrontation. According to *Changing for Good*, "Most people in the preparation stage are planning to take action."[37] Also it is said, "The action stage is one in which people most overtly modify their behavior and their surroundings."[38] It takes courage to act in spite of fear of failure or the lack of success in the past.

Job wanted to hear from God so he would know what to do to get back to where he was before messengers started showing up at his home with bad news. His encounter with God went beyond reasoning by asking

---

[37] Prochaska, *Changing for Good*, 43.

[38] Ibid., 44.

questions he could not answer that drew attention to his imperfect knowledge. Job was suffering in every way imaginable. He lost his family, friends, and fortune.

Instead of fixing everything that was broken in Job's life, he witnessed another storm. While still suffering and "from the eye of [another] violent storm," the Lord answered Job's questions with a question. The Lord asked, "Who is this that obscures my plans with words without knowledge?" (Job 38:2, NIV) Notice that this weather event was not only intense but it was large enough to have an eye. It is amazing that the Lord and the storm are mentioned together. Because Job heard the Lord's voice coming from the storm, we can infer that the storm did not end when the Lord showed up.

Churnai quotes from Kathleen O'Connor's essay *Considering Job* when she states, "The storm evokes Job's own stormy life whipped about within and without by chaotic forces. The storm, thus, represents theological conflict and the resolution of the book."[39] Churnai explains, "Two speeches of Yahweh function as instruction. They use the non-human world to provide knowledge about the human world."[40] She acknowledges, "Some insights and implications of his dreadful suffering and death are put together and made available for Job."[41] Given an opportunity, God asked Job if he still wanted to argue his case. It feels like he was warning Job that he was about to be asked questions that he could not answer. Churnai points out, "God's unanswerable

---

[39] Churnai, *Beyond Justice*, loc. 3192.

[40] Ibid., loc. 3208.

[41] Ibid.

questions are to remind Job the inequalities between him and God. God is God, and Job is a creature."[42]

Job confronted the realization that his determination and willpower had limits. In chapters 3, 13, and 23, Job seemed to be anxious to bargain with the Lord when he presented a record of his life – as if the Lord needed to be told. Job provided weighty rebuttals to every argument laid out by his friends. His friends shared from their exhaustive knowledge and understanding. However, Job needed to hear from the Lord. Suffering can create an insatiable desire to hear the sound of His voice. The psalmist cries, "Hear my voice when I call, LORD; be merciful to me and answer me." (Ps. 27:7, NIV)

There is no indication as to how long Job and his friends pontificated possible explanations for Job's suffering. They had been sitting and debating over an extensive period of time. Elihu challenged Job when he insisted, "Answer me then, if you can; stand up and argue your case before me." (Job 33:5, NIV) In other words, Elihu gave Job an opportunity to rehearse the case for self-righteousness that he would present to the Lord. To do so, Job would need to confront the inherent risk of coming into the presence of the Lord who could either destroy Job as if he were an enemy or discipline Job like he was a child.

Job's young friend, Elihu, could wait no longer and spoke eloquently when he said, "At this my heart pounds and leaps from its place. God's voice thunders in marvelous ways; he does great things beyond our understanding." (Job 37:1, 5 NIV) At just the right time, when it seemed they were exhausted and emotionally drained, "The Lord spoke to Job out of the storm." (Job 38:1) I find comfort in this passage because it shows that the Prince of Peace and storms can be in the same place at the same time.

---

[42] Ibid., loc. 3437.

Churnai explains this confrontation by saying, "[Job] has accused God of being unjust (i.e. according to the view of divine justice in the retribution principle) and challenges God's moral right to rule the world. Thus God wants Job to reconsider what constitutes justice ('my justice,' Job 40:8)."[43] Churnai goes on to say,

> "God, who has been considered unjust by Job, challenges Job to govern the world and to show that he has the integrity and power to control the wicked. If Job can do that, God will honor him." (Job 40:14) To demonstrate to Job his ignorance and impotence, God singles out two primordial forces of chaos for Job's special consideration: Behemoth (Job 40:15-24) and Leviathan (Job 41:1-34).[44]

The process of grieving helped to prepare Job to hear from the Lord and be reminded of His greatness. Instead of looking forward to telling the Lord about the injustice he was enduring, Job was prepared to listen. In despair, Job may have thought his relationship with the Lord was severed. Churnai states, "God's revelation is not to punish Job or put him down, but to summon, not because of Job's claim, but a gracious and loving revelation."[45]

In the first chapters of Job, the narrator lets readers know what Satan planned for Job. However, we had no idea what the Lord had planned for Job or his wife or his friends. During Job's encounter with the Lord, we will see how the grieving process played a role in changing his mind about what to expect from God. Job was also transformed into a powerful and effective

---

[43] Churnai, *Beyond Justice*, loc. 3483.

[44] Ibid., loc. 3499.

[45] Ibid.

intercessor. In spite of their contentious discussions and conflicting expla-nations for Job's predicament, grieving completed its work in them and they were reconciled to the Lord.

CHAPTER 6

Transformation Matters

"It doesn't matter whether we have been circumcised or not. What counts is whether we have been transformed into a new creation." Gal. 6:15, NLT

To be transformed is to become new in every respect. Job was changed. He had a new understanding about God. Job would never be the same. Given an opportunity to reflect on his suffering, it was evident that his perspective of suffering had changed.

Transformation could compare to reaching maintenance in the Stages of Change. Getting to that point would be an indication that a level of success had been reached in the early stages. Prochaska, Norcross, and DiClemente write, "It is during maintenance that [one] must work to consolidate the gains attained during the action and other stages, and struggle to prevent lapses and relapse."[46] Metamorphosis is a familiar biological term often used to describe the transformation of a caterpillar into a beautiful butterfly. Unlike a maintenance relapse that may occur in the Stages of Change, butterflies can never become caterpillars again. In contrast,

---

[46] Prochaska, *Changing for Good*, 45.

transformation is not a destination. It is a process. Job's body was a living sacrifice to God's will. The good, pleasing, and perfect will of God for Job would ultimately be revealed.

A Theory of Grieving was applied to this study of Job's suffering to help us understand that we can choose to work through difficulties rather than let our difficulties derail personal transformation. The transformation of Job and his friends would be lasting. It really mattered that Job was changed emotionally, physically, and spiritually. Following his period of suffering and grieving, Job's sense of entitlement changed. Job's reverence and fear of the Lord changed. Job's level of piety changed. The change in Job extended to Eliphaz, Bildad, Zophar, and Elihu. They were transformed because their knowledge and understanding of God was no longer based on what they had experienced in the past. While they were comforting and consoling Job, they were blessed to experience new grace and new mercy from the Sovereign Lord.

In Job chapter 42, it is apparent that Job's disposition toward his suffering was transformed. He learned things about the Lord that he might not have found out without going through the grieving and the suffering associated with such tremendous crises.

Job listened to his friends for a while before he said, "But I desire to speak to the Almighty and to argue my case with God." (Job 3:13, NIV) However, Job was unable to speak when the Lord questioned him in chapters 38 through 40. The Lord asked, "Would you discredit my justice? Would you condemn me to justify yourself?" (Job 40:8, NIV) Job was challenged to no longer weigh justice on the scale of retribution. He knew that God's plans transcended earthly justice. Now Job knows what William Mounce explains, "God has the power to transform things from one reality to another."[47]

---

[47] Mounce, *Mounce's Dictionary*, "transform."

The Lord reminded Job that all of creation was indebted to him for its existence. He asked, "Who has a claim against me that I must pay? Everything under heaven belongs to me." (Job 41:11, NIV) Job no longer had a desire to question God. Hearing God and seeing his manifestation out of a storm transformed Job's opinion of himself. Apparently, Job was less pious and more humble when he proclaimed, "My ears had heard of you but now my eyes have seen you. Therefore, I despise myself and repent in dust and ashes." (Job 42:5-6, NIV)

Similar to the termination Stage of Change, Job's suffering ended. Churnai concludes by saying, "Job acknowledges his finitude and mortality. Job finds himself as dying to his old self. He is transformed in his self-understanding after the second divine speech."[48] Job would never be the same and admitted to knowing seven things. First, he told the Lord, "I know that you can do all things; no purpose of yours can be thwarted." (Job 42:2, NIV) Before Job got in trouble, he had a mental grasp of the Lord as a provider and protector. His experience enlarged his understanding so that he was conscious of the Lord's great power. In contrast to what the Lord did in the beginning by forming nothing into something and filling

---

[48] Churnai, *Beyond Justice*, loc. 3772.

it with everything, Job was asked where he was when all of that happened. There was no comparison.

Second, Job has a better understanding of power and purpose. The word thwart is useful in this context because it suggests power being employed to intentionally oppose, frustrate, and prevent easy explanations for complex issues. Just imagine Satan's frustration when Job did not yield to his wife's temptation to curse God. Even when Job welcomed death, the power was not in his hands. Pressure from his friends and the pain from his sickness did not prevent him from praising the Lord.

This lesson is affirmed in other biblical examples of opposition being overcome. The anointed – but not appointed — king David remembered when he was hiding in a cave from Saul and wrote, "I cry out to God Most High, to God who will fulfill his purpose for me." (Ps. 57:2, NLT) Danger appeared to delay David's destiny. In spite of opposition, God kept his covenant and David's purpose was fulfilled.

The Lord let the prophet Jeremiah know that there was a purpose for Babylonian captivity when He said, "And I will give them one heart and one purpose: to worship me forever, for their own good and for the good of all their descendants." (Jer. 32:39, NLT) We see in Job 1:5 that he worshipped the Lord on purpose because he knew it was good for him and his children.

Third, Job continues, "You asked, 'Who is this that obscures my plans without knowledge?' Surely I spoke of things I did not understand, things too wonderful for me to know." (Job 42:3, NIV) Job and his friends realize they did not know what they did not know. They had no idea what the Lord had in store for them. The apostle Paul wrote in the New Testament, "That is what the Scriptures mean when they say, 'No eye has seen, no ear has heard, and no mind has imagined what God has prepared for those who love him.'" (1 Cor. 2:9, NLT)

Grievers and skilled grief caregivers must learn to rely on the verses that say, "Trust in the LORD with all your heart and lean not on your own understanding; in all your ways submit to him, and he will make your paths straight. Do not be wise in your own eyes; fear the LORD and shun evil." (Prov. 3:5-7, NIV)

Fourth, Job imagined what it would be like to argue his case in the Lord's presence. He claimed,

> "I would state my case before him and fill my mouth with arguments. I would find out what he would answer me, and consider what he would say to me. Would he vigorously oppose me? No, he would not press charges against me. There the upright can establish their innocence before him, and there I would be delivered forever from my judge." (Job 23:4-7, NIV)

Job and his friends did not realize that court was already in session and the Lord was listening. Not only is there a time for everything, but there could be a time limit, also. There is a time to talk and there is a time to listen. Job let the Lord know that he understood what time it was when he repeated, "You said, 'Listen now, and I will speak; I will question you, and you shall answer me.'" (Job 42:4, NIV) It was time for the Lord to turn the conversation around.

Fifth, Job was willing to be quiet during the pain of being criticized by Eliphaz. Job expected to learn from this problem. He was open to learning from nature. He was willing to turn to animals, birds, or even fish if they could possibly help him figure out why he was experiencing such staggering suffering. At one point Elihu called himself a teacher and insisted that everyone give him their attention. He turns to Job and challenges him to teach them about God. Job is directed, "Tell us what we should say to him;

we cannot draw up our case because of our darkness." (Job 37:19, NIV) Job asked, "Can anyone teach knowledge to God, since he judges even the highest?" (Job 21:22, NIV) He concluded that no one could teach God since he is the supreme judge.

Sixth, Job knows that the Lord will reveal himself when the time is right. After the youthful Elihu waited patiently to speak, he got excited as he thought about the presence of God. To him, the voice of God sounded like thunder that rolled and roared from his mouth without restraint giving direction to the snow and the rain. "The stormy wind comes from its chamber, and the driving winds bring the cold." (Job 37:9, NLT) Elihu continues to talk about God's control over the lightning, clouds, and sun. Even with all that power, the Lord Almighty does not destroy us.

Elihu spoke of storms that could speak to all the earth. He concluded by saying, "No wonder people everywhere fear him. All who are wise show him reverence." (37:24, NLT) It is hard to ignore a storm with a voice. Job declared, "My ears had heard of you but now my eyes have seen you." (Job 42:5, NIV)

Finally, it is evident that Job has been transformed when he repents in Job 42:1-6. His condition has not changed but he reconciles with his friends in Job 42:7-9. He is not restored until Job 42:10-17. When Job saw the Lord, he realized the need to repent. Churnai states, "The rejection of the retribution principle allowed Job to behold the gracious face of God. Job is called to simply trust in God's mercy, in his graciousness and compassion, even in the face of undeserved suffering and imminent death."[49] Gustavo Gutierrez stated, "God is always present to help us in darkness and despair. His strong hand is filled with grace and mercy. Job ... flung himself upon the impossible and into an enigmatic future. And in this effort he met the Lord."[50]

---

[49] Ibid., loc. 684.

[50] Gutierrez, God-Talk, 92.

This study applied *A Theory of Grieving* to help us see how Job, his wife, and his friends assessed crises, acknowledged conflict, assimilated considerations, and accelerated confrontation. In Job's times of trouble, he did not think he was better than he was; he was honest in his evaluation of himself; and he was unshakeable in the measure of faith God had given him. Job was transformed and he let God change the way he thought. Job learned to know God's will for him and trust him. Again, we are advised, "Don't copy the behavior and customs of this world, but let God transform you into a new person by changing the way you think. Then you will learn to know God's will for you, which is good, pleasing, and perfect." (Rom. 12:2, NLT) It can be comforting to know that we are being transformed with every crisis.

Epilogue

"This same Good News that came to you is going out all over the world. It is bearing fruit everywhere by changing lives, just as it changed your lives from the day you first heard and understood the truth about God's wonderful grace." Col. 1:6, NLT

Exploring Job's crises allowed us to see into the life of someone who was suffering. Those who are grieving, mourning, bereaved, or in trouble may discover some timeless truths in Job's search for answers. He needed to be comforted while he survived the pain and you may have that same need. When it was the right time for Job, the Lord made His presence known. In their conversation with the Lord, Job and his friends realized the Lord was with them all the time. It is comforting to read, "The righteous cry out, and the LORD hears them; he delivers them from all their troubles." (Ps. 34:17, NIV) The Lord responds to our pain. He forgives and restores.

Job's friends set an example that we can follow. The narrator makes some closing remarks, "So Eliphaz the Temanite, Bildad the Shuhite and Zophar the Naamathite did what the LORD told them; and the LORD accepted Job's prayer. After Job had prayed for his friends, the LORD restored his fortunes and gave him twice as much as he had before." (Job 42:9-10, NIV) Grief caregivers must be sensitive to the Lord's direction; do what the Lord tells them to do; and pray for one another.

Gutierrez says, "We have accompanied Job as his experience of unjust suffering broadened and he acquired a moving realization of the suffering of others."[51] There is evidence that grieving contributed to the transformation of Job and his friends. Grieving can help change the way we think about crises that sometime come in the form of trouble, trials, or tribulations. We are reminded, "Dear brothers and sisters, when troubles of any kind come your way, consider it an opportunity for great joy." (James 1:2, NLT) Suffering and loss put Job's faith to the test. Even though he did not know the Lord's plans for him, the principles of *A Theory of Grief* can be observed as he was being transformed. Not only was he able to endure constant accusations from his friends, but he stood firm. Job was a man who did not waver and remained loyal. When he was unsettled by trouble, he was secure enough in his faith to persist and praise his way through his problems. He spent a lot of time just sitting with his situation. Job confessed to knowing more about the Lord after he came through the trouble.

Grieving can help transform the way we think about treasure. Satan was sure that Job only served the Lord because he received material blessings. Job questioned himself about what made him feel safe. Job searched himself and asked, "Have I put my trust in money or felt secure because of my gold? Have I gloated about my wealth and all that I own?" (Job 31:24-25, NLT) Job was humble but confident that he could successfully defend himself against accusations of any kind. He said, "I would face the accusation proudly. I would wear it like a crown. For I would tell him

---

[51] Gutierrez, *On Job: God-Talk and the Suffering of the Innocent*, 93.

exactly what I have done. I would come before him like a prince." (Job 31:36-37, NLT)

Grieving can help transform the way we think about tests. When our faith is tested, endurance has a chance to grow and be developed. Peter wrote,

> "Trials will show that your faith is genuine. It is being tested as fire tests and purifies gold—though your faith is far more precious than mere gold. So when your faith remains strong through many trials, it will bring you much praise and glory and honor on the day when Jesus Christ is revealed to the whole world."
>
> 1 Pet. 1:7, NLT

Jeremiah entreated, "O Lord of Heaven's Armies, you test those who are righteous, and examine the deepest thoughts and secrets. Let me see your vengeance against them, for I have committed my cause to you."(Jer. 20:12, NLT) Job trusted in the Lord and attested, "But he knows where I am going. And when he tests me, I will come out as pure gold." (Job 23:10, NLT) It is only after being tested that we can be perfect, complete, and need nothing.

Grieving can help us learn to know God's will for us. Of course, the pressing question for Job and his friends was, "Why is this God's will for me at this time?" We know that trouble, trials, and tests help us mature emotionally and spiritually. We learn to trust in the Love of God. Using the principles of *A Theory of Grief* can help us stand firm and confess, "For I am convinced that neither death nor life, neither angels nor demons, neither the present nor the future, nor any powers, neither height nor depth, nor anything else in all creation, will be able to separate us from the love of God that is in Christ Jesus our Lord." (Rom. 8:38-39, NIV) Satan had to be extremely disappointed in Job.

This study revealed that crises provide the crucible for change that brings about transformation. The specifics may change but the purpose remains the same. Four passages of scripture support this conclusion. First, we assert, "All Scripture is God-breathed and is useful for teaching, rebuking, correcting and training in righteousness, so that the servant of God may be thoroughly equipped for every good work." (2 Tim. 3:16-17, NIV) Not knowing or understanding the reason seemed to compound Job's suffering. Job said to Eliphaz, "Teach me, and I will be quiet; show me where I have been wrong." (Job 6:24, NIV) We sense Job's desperation when he asked his friend for answers no one had. Job was seeking information that would point to his fault, lead him to repentance, cause him to be reconciled to the Lord, and be more disciplined in blameless living. Job wanted the nightmare to end.

Grief and suffering are not restricted to those who know scripture — or even know about it. "Scholars have traditionally placed the events of [Job] in the patriarchal period, citing the absence of any reference to covenant or law."[52] Somehow he came to know enough about God that he worshipped and praised him all the time. Studying Job emphasized how important it is for the church to use biblical principles skillfully to meet the needs of those who suffer from the myriad of losses. We want them to know that the Lord is near the brokenhearted.

Job gives one of the clearest views of Spiritual Warfare between Satan and the Lord. Satan was looking for a fight and the Lord served it up to him. Job could be called the prequel to Judah being taken into Babylonian captivity. The second scripture is taken from the prophet Jeremiah's letter from the Lord to the southern kingdom of Judah prior to their being taken

---

[52] *NIV Cultural Background Study Bible*, 824.

into Babylonian captivity. It reads, "For I know the plans I have for you," declares the LORD, "plans to prosper you and not to harm you, plans to give you hope and a future." (Jer. 29:11, NIV) The prophet Jeremiah's letter to Judah reminded them that Babylonian captivity was inevitable because they refused to change from idol worship to the God of their salvation. Force was used to change them and punish them. However, they were not confined arbitrarily. There was a plan. Their captivity would be difficult and include threats of harm, but the result would be prosperity. The promised outcome was the gift of hope they would need to pursue their future.

In the meantime, the people would have to follow instructions and do their part without knowing all the details in advance. In essence, the Lord was addressing Judah's anticipatory grief. To summarize Jeremiah chapter 29:4-10, the people were instructed to make the best of a bad situation. They were to build houses, plant gardens, get married, have children, increase in number, seek peace and prosperity of the city. They were told not to listen to prophesying lies. They would be suffering for no less than seventy years. They were told when their captivity would end. It was not easy for them to wait for such a long time without a whisper from the Lord. Just like they learned that God was faithful, Job was fully persuaded that God could be trusted. We have evidence that the Lord had plans for whatever his people went through.

Third, at some point, everyone will be confronted with the reality of change or losses due to a current, imminent, anticipated, or inevitable crisis. Again, Proverbs states,

> "Trust GOD from the bottom of your heart; don't try to figure out everything on your own. Listen for GOD's voice in everything you do, everywhere you go; he's the one who will keep you on track. Don't assume that you know it all. Run to GOD!

Run from evil! Your body will glow with health, your very bones will vibrate with life!"

Prov. 3:5-8, MSG

All human beings are exposed to suffering either up close or from a distance. Knowing what to expect and being sensitive to signs of bereavement could facilitate spiritual and emotional healing. Sometime attempts to console one another with familiar scriptures actually give rise to conflict between faith and feelings. Care must be taken that selected verses do not discount, discourage, or ignore how grievers are behaving. It is difficult to reconcile anger, bargaining, depression, frustration, and guilt with unshakeable faith and the inseparable love of God. The change may be gradual but the evidence ultimately becomes recognizable.

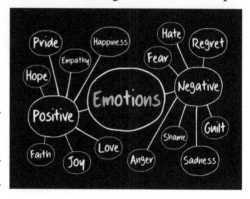

Finally, change is the desired outcome. Konigsberg says, "Most people are resilient enough to get through loss and reach an acceptable level of adjustment on their own."[53] However, sitting with Job and sharing in his grief allowed time for emotional, social, and spiritual care — holistic ministry. Churnai concludes that "in the book of Job there is no affirmation that the scale of divine justice will be balanced in the afterlife; the emphasis is on trusting in the graciousness of God without demanding an answer, even when God's graciousness and mercy seem to be hidden."[54]

---

[53] Ruth Davis Konigsberg, *The Truth about Grief: The Myth of Its Five Stages and the New Science of Loss,* (New York: Simon and Schuster, 2011), 198.

[54] Churnai, *Beyond Justice,* loc. 4284.

"Christ [came] to give us a new way of thinking — not to legalistically follow a fixed set of rules and regulations, but to desire to serve Jesus with all our heart and mind."[55] Writing and talking were powerful tools that provided ways for introspection, reflection, and correction so that Job and his friends could increase their knowledge and understanding of the sovereignty, character, and love of God. Job demonstrated, like God, that he was gracious and kind when he did not have to be. He sacrificed and prayed for his friends in spite of their failed attempts to comfort and console him. God's grace and kindness goes beyond justice.

Job [went] beyond justice in social and conventional practice with his treatment of his daughters."[56] After suffering, Job demonstrated a transformed understanding of equality. We are told, "Nowhere in all the land were there found women as beautiful as Job's daughters, and their father granted them an inheritance along with their brothers." (Job 42:15, NIV) After Job was transformed, he changed the way he thought about his wealth. He changed and he transformed the future for his daughters.

Job and his friends learned that God's sovereignty superseded retribution theology. God established a relationship with His people that is not based on transactions. Job's suffering turned into an opportunity for a deeper revelation of God's love, grace, and mercy. Job grew in his knowledge and understanding of God's power, presence, plans, and purpose for his life.

---

[55] Mounce, *Mounce's Complete Expository Dictionary*, "transform."

[56] Churnai, *Beyond Justice*, Kindle 3908

In Loving Memory of My *"Mo Dear"*

Ruth Ella James Rosborough Hood

Questions and Discussions Regarding Grief

"These trials will show that your faith is genuine. It is being tested as fire tests and purifies gold—though your faith is far more precious than mere gold. So when your faith remains strong through many trials, it will bring you much praise and glory and honor on the day when Jesus Christ is revealed to the whole world."

1 Pet. 1:7, NLT

1. Assess the crises **JOB** experienced in Job 1:1-3, 13-19; and 2:7.

A. DEATH:
___People ___Pets ___Dreams
___Divorce ___Reproduction ___Distress
___Relationships

B. DISEASE:
___Diagnosis ___Pain ___Poor Health
___Treatments ___Chronic Illness ___Caregiver Obligations

C. DISABILITY:
___Physical ___Emotional ___Financial
___From Birth ___Mobility ___Limitations
___Restrictions ___Unexpected Challenges

D. DEFICIT:
___Deprivation ___Food ___Clothes
___Shelter ___Finances ___Peace
___Unmet Needs

E. DECISIONS:
___Stay/Go ___Yes/No ___Speak/Silence
___Discipline ___Worry ___Lack of Control

F. DESTRUCTION:
___Disaster ___Accident ___Abuse
___Injustice ___Incarceration ___Mass Casualties

2. Asses the crises **You** have experienced in the last few years. These choices are not exhaustive.

A.	DEATH:	___People	___Pets	___Dreams
		___Divorce	___Reproduction	___Distress
		___Relationships		

B.	DISEASE:	___Diagnosis	___Pain	___Poor Health
		___Treatments	___Chronic Illness	___Caregiver Obligations

C.	DISABILITY:	___Physical	___Emotional	___Financial
		___From Birth	___Mobility	___Limitations
		___Restrictions	___Unexpected Challenges	

D.	DEFICIT:	___Deprivation	___Food	___Clothes
		___Shelter	___Finances	___Peace
		___Unmet Needs		

E.	DECISIONS:	___Stay/Go	___Yes/No	___Speak/Silence
		___Discipline	___Worry	___Lack of Control

F.	DESTRUCTION:	___Disaster	___Accident	___Abuse
		___Injustice	___Incarceration	___Mass Casualties

3. After reading **Job** 1:1-2:10 from NIV/NLT/MSG, identify Job's losses using the information from Maslow's Hierarchy of Human Needs.

A. PHYSICAL:

___Air   ___Food   ___Water

___Shelter   ___Clothing   ___Sleep

___Reproduction

B. SAFETY & SECURITY:

___Trust   ___Boundaries

___Employment   ___Safety from Injury

___Secure neighborhoods   ___Health and Wellness

___Property Ownership   ___Social Ability

___Family   ___Stability

C. LOVE & BELONGING:

___Family   ___Friendship

___Connections   ___Love and Intimacy

          ___Social/Religious/Community Belonging

___Respect **for** others   ___Acceptance

D. SELF-ESTEEM:

___Confidence   ___Appreciation

___Individuality   ___Respect **of** others

___Connections   ___Achievements/Accomplishments

___Purpose Driven

E. SELF-ACTUALIZATION:

___Morality   ___Creativity

___Acceptance   ___Spontaneity

___Fulfillment   ___Reach Potential

___Self-awareness   ___Personal Growth

4. Identify losses that **You** experienced in the last few years. These choices are not exhaustive.

A. PHYSICAL:

    ___Air   ___Food   ___Water

    ___Shelter   ___Clothing   ___Sleep

    ___Reproduction

B. SAFETY & SECURITY:

    ___Trust   ___Boundaries

    ___Employment   ___Safety from Injury

    ___Secure neighborhoods   ___Health and Wellness

    ___Property Ownership   ___Social Ability

    ___Family   ___Stability

C. LOVE & BELONGING:

    ___Family   ___Friendship

    ___Connections   ___Love and Intimacy

    ___Social/Religious/Community Belonging

    ___Respect **for** others   ___Acceptance

D. SELF-ESTEEM:

    ___Confidence   ___Appreciation

    ___Individuality   ___Respect **of** others

    ___Connections   ___Achievements/Accomplishments

    ___Purpose Driven

E. SELF-ACTUALIZATION:

    ___Morality   ___Creativity

    ___Acceptance   ___Spontaneity

    ___Fulfillment   ___Reach Potential

    ___Self-awareness   ___Personal Growth

5. After reading **Job** 1:20-22; 2:8-3:26 from NIV/NLT/MSG, identify the emotions Job expressed in response to his crises and losses.

A. BLISSFUL:

___Extreme Happiness   ___Festive   ___Ecstatic

___Rapture   ___Euphoria   ___Exaltation

___Supreme   ___Well Being   ___Glee

B. GLAD:

___Joyful   ___Cheerful   ___Happy

___Pleased   ___Grateful   ___Hopeful

___In Good Spirits   ___Hopeful   ___Proud   ___Faithful

C. BALANCED:

___Content   ___At Peace   ___Satisfied

___Not Anxious   ___Not Angry   ___Acceptance

___Fulfilled   ___Grateful   ___At Ease

D. SAD:

___Discouraged   ___Dissatisfied   ___Disappointed

___Guilty   ___Miserable   ___Sorry

___Ashamed   ___Pitiful   ___Disconsolate

___Discontent   ___Regretful

E. ANGER:

___Offended   ___Frustrated   ___Uptight

___Indignant   ___Resentful   ___Annoyed

___Aggravated   ___Exasperated   ___Bitter

___Hate   ___Irate

6. Reflect on **Your** emotional response to crises and losses that **you** experienced in the last few years.

A. BLISSFUL:

___Extreme Happiness   ___Festive   ___Ecstatic

___Rapture   ___Euphoria   ___Exaltation

___Supreme   ___Well Being   ___Glee

B. GLAD:

___Joyful   ___Cheerful   ___Happy

___Pleased   ___Grateful   ___Hopeful

___In Good Spirits   ___Hopeful   ___Proud   ___Faithful

C. BALANCED:

___Content   ___At Peace   ___Satisfied

___Not Anxious   ___Not Angry   ___Acceptance

___Fulfilled   ___Grateful   ___At Ease

D. SAD:

___Discouraged   ___Dissatisfied   ___Disappointed

___Guilty   ___Miserable   ___Sorry

___Ashamed   ___Pitiful   ___Disconsolate

___Discontent   ___Regretful

E. ANGER:

___Offended   ___Frustrated   ___Uptight

___Indignant   ___Resentful   ___Annoyed

___Aggravated   ___Exasperated   ___Bitter

___Hate   ___Irate

7. Refer to Chapter 3 and react to the discussion about Job's wife.

8. Refer to Chapter 4 and discuss the role of Retribution Theology in grief care.

9. Refer to Chapter 4 and discuss which friend you consider a model grief caregiver.

10. Refer to Chapter 5 and discuss the arguments Job used to confront his frustrations and fears.

11. Refer to Chapter 6 and discuss how Job and his friends were transformed as they shared in Job's suffering.

12. Discuss your reaction to the Epilogue.

Discuss whether you AGREE or DISAGREE with the following statements based on Ephesians 3:13-19 from the New Living Translation:

13. Grieving can help us grow stronger hearts: As servant evangelists, we can show that Grief matters so that people do not lose heart because of their trials. Even though we do not suffer for others, we should feel honored to suffer with them. When we think of all the suffering, we fall to our knees and pray to the Father, the Creator of everything in heaven and on earth. We pray that from his glorious, unlimited resources he will empower us with inner strength through his Spirit.

14. Grieving can help us grow deeper roots: Grieving opens the door for Christ to make his home in your hearts as you trust in him. Your roots

will grow down into God's love and keep you strong. In addition, may you have the power to understand, as all God's people should, how wide, how long, how high, and how deep his love is.

15. Grieving can help us grow to fullness: Grieving is a time to experience the love of Christ, though it is too great to understand fully. After you have grieved for a while, then you will be complete with all the fullness of life and power that comes from God.

Glossary

The following definitions of key terms are used throughout this book::

A Theory of Grieving. This principle is like a tool kit of skills that could be helpful as one is in process of transformation.

Adversity. This term describes a state of hardship, affliction, or misfortune. A calamitous event has extreme unfortunate or dire consequences bringing ruin or instability.

Bereaved. This term describes sorrow experienced or expressed because of irreparable loss, change, or deprivation.

Change. This term means to cause to be different or go from one phase to another.

Comfort. This term conveys reassurance and soothing consolation by bringing solace or cheer to another.

Compassion. This term describes the feeling of deep sympathy and sorrow for someone affected by crises accompanied by a desire to alleviate the pain and suffering.

Conflict. This term describes what may seem like an irreconcilable struggle, emotional disturbance, or clash between feelings, facts, and faith.

Confront. This term describes facing risks and barriers to moving beyond current circumstances. Taking action may have positive or negative consequences.

Consider. This term refers to weighing information deliberately and carefully for relevance, strengths, weaknesses, and limitations in forming a judgment or making a decision.

Crisis. This term describes the wide range of trouble, trials, tribulations, and tests that cause physical, emotional, relational, or financial instability.

Grief. This term refers to normal and natural responses to bereavement, separation, loss, or trouble due to a current, imminent, anticipated, or inevitable change.

Loss. This term describes the condition of being deprived or bereft of something or someone; the harm or suffering caused by losing; or consequences from needs not being met.

Mourn. This term refers to feeling, showing, or expressing grief.

Prosper. This term refers to being healthy in body, strong in spirit, and successful on life's journey.

Reconciliation. This term refers to "the removal of enmity and the restoration of fellowship between two parties."[57]

Redemption. This term refers to "Christ's saving work viewed as an act of buying back sinners out of their bondage to sin and to Satan through payment of a ransom."[58]

---

[57] Wayne Grudem, *Systematic Theology: An Introduction to Biblical Doctrine*, (Grand Rapids: Zondervan, 1994), 1253.

[58] Ibid.

Restoration. This term refers to the replacement or giving back of something lost, something replaced, or something reconstructed.

Soul. This term refers to the immaterial aspects of life, feelings, or inner self (see Rom. 7:22; Eph. 3:16). The soul consists of mind (what you think), will (what you do), and emotions (what you feel).

Suffer. This term means to feel the pain or distress of sustaining loss, injury, harm, or punishment.

Transformation. This term refers to change in appearance, character, or function that goes beyond reformation. The result may be conviction, conversion, alteration, repentance, redemption, reconciliation, reconstruction, or restoration.

Bibliography

Beale, G. K. *Handbook on the New Testament Use of the Old Testament.* Grand Rapids: Baker Academic, 2012.

Block, Daniel Isaac. *Judges, Ruth.* New American Commentary. Nashville: Broadman & Holman, 1999.

_____, 2015. *Ruth.* Exegetical Commentary on the Old Testament. Grand Rapids: Zondervan.

Blomberg, Craid. *Matthew.* The New American Commentary. Nashville: Broadman, 1992.

Churnai, Varunaj. *Beyond Justice: Death and the Retribution Principle in the Book of Job.* Carlisle, UK: Langham Monograhs, 2018.

Clinebell, Howard. *Basic Types of Pastoral Care & Counseling: Resources for the Ministry of Healing and Growth.* Nashville: Abingdon, 1984.

Clinton, Tim, Archibald Hart and George Ohlschlager, eds. *Caring for People God's Way: Personal and Emotional Issues, Addictions, Grief, and Trauma.* Nashville: Nelson, 2005.

Davids, Peter H. *The First Epistle of Peter.* Grand Rapids: Eerdmans, 1990.

Davidson, Glen W., *Understanding Mourning: A Guide for Those Who Grieve.* Minneapolis: Augsburg, 1984.

Enduring Word. "Bethlehem to Moab, Ruth 1:1." Accessed March 29, 2019. https://enduringword.com/bible-commentary/ruth-1/.

France, R.T. *The Gospel According to Matthew: An Introduction and Commentary.* Grand Rapids: Eerdmans, 1985.

Franklin, Benjamin. *Poor Richard's Almanac.* Edited by Benjamin E. Smith. New York: Century, 1898.

Gappelt, Leonhardt, Ferdinand Hahn, and John E. Alsup. *A Commentary on 1 Peter.* Grand Rapids: Eerdmans, 1993.

Grudem, Wayne. *Systematic Theology: An Introduction to Biblical Doctrine.* Grand Rapids: Zondervan, 1994.

Gutierrez, Gustavo. *On Job: God-talk and the Suffering of the Innocent.* Maryknoll, NY: Orbis Books, 1987.

Hafermann, Scott J. *2 Corinthians The NIV Application Commentary from Biblical Text to Contemporary Life.* Grand Rapids: Zondervan, 2000.

Hagner, Donald Alfred. *Matthew 1-13.* Word Biblical Commentary. Dallas: Word, 1993.

Hals, Ronald M. *The Theology of the Book of Ruth.* Philadelphia: Fortress, 1969.

Hill, Andrew E., and John H. Walton. *A Survey of the Old Testament*, 2nd ed. Grand Rapids: Zondervan, 2000.

Holmstedt, Robert D. *Ruth: A Handbook on the Hebrew Text.* Baylor Handbook on the Hebrew Bible Series. Waco, TX: Baylor University Press, 2010.

Hubbard, Robert L., Jr. *The Book of Ruth*. New International Commentary on the Old Testament. Grand Rapids: Eerdmans, 1988.

Jackman, David. *Judges, Ruth*. The Communicator's Commentary. Dallas: Word, 1991.

James, John W., and Russell Friedman. *The Grief Recovery Handbook*. New York: HarperCollins, 2009.

Kaiser, Walter. *Grief and Pain in the Plan of God: Christian Assurance and the Message of Lamentations*. Fearn, Scotland: Christian Focus, 2004.

Keener, Craig S. And John H. Watson, *NIV Cultural Backgrounds Study Bible*. Grand Rapids: Zondervan, 2016.

Konigsberg, Ruth Davis. *The Truth about Grief: The Myth of Its Five Stages and the New Science of Loss*. New York: Simon and Schuster, 2011.

Kübler-Ross, Elisabeth. *On Death and Dying: What the Dying Have to Teach Doctors, Nurses, Clergy & Their Own Families*. New York: Scribner, 2019.

Lange, John Peter, and Philip Schaff. *A Commentary on the Holy Scriptures: Critical, Doctrinal, and Homiletical*. Grand Rapids: Zondervan, 1960.

Martin, Ralph P. *2 Corinthians*. World Biblical Commentary. Waco, TX: Word, 1986.

Maslow, A. H. *A Theory of Human Motivation*. Connecticut: Martino Publishing, 2013.

Metzger, Bruce, David Allan Hubbard, and Glenn W. Barker. *Word Biblical Commentary*, vol. 13. Waco, TX: Word, 2011.

Milazzo, G. Tom. *The Protest and the Silence: Suffering, Death, and Biblical Theology*. Minneapolis: Fortress, 1992.

Moo, Douglas J. *The Epistle to the Romans*. Grand Rapids: Eerdmans, 1996.

Moore, R. Kelvin. *The Psalms of Lamentation and the Enigma of Suffering*. Lewiston, NY: Mellen, 1996.

Morgan, Christopher W., and Robert A. Peterson. *Suffering and the Goodness of God*. Wheaton, IL: Crossway, 2008.

Mounce, William D., ed. *Mounce's Complete Expository Dictionary of Old and New Testament Words*. Grand Rapids: Zondervan, 2006.

Osborne, Grant R. *Matthew*. Exegetical Commentary on the New Testament. Grand Rapids: Zondervan, 2010.

Peak, Arthur. *The Problem of Suffering in the Old Testament*. London: Epworth, 1947.

Piper, John, and Justin Taylor, eds. *Suffering and the Sovereignty of God*. Wheaton, IL: Crossway, 2006.

Prochaska, James O, John C. Norcross and Carlo C. DiClemente. *Changing for Good*. New York: HarperCollins, 2006.

Prochaska, James O, and Janice M. Prochaska. *Changing to Thrive*. Center City: Hazelden, 2016.

Reid, Alvin L, and David A. Wheeler. *Servant Evangelism: Showing and Sharing the Good News*. Illinois: Gospel Advance Books, 2013.

Richard, Lucien. *What are They Saying about the Theology of Suffering?* New York: Paulist, 1992.

Schreiner, Thomas R. *Romans*. Grand Rapids: Baker, 1998.

Smith, Robert Houston, and Charles M. Laymon. *Old Testament History: A Commentary on Joshua, Judges, Ruth, I and II Samuel, I and II Kings, I and II Chronicles, Ezra, Nehemiah, Esther.* Nashville: Abingdon, 1983.

Stott, John R.W. *Romans: God's Good News for the World.* Chicago: Inter-Varsity Press, 1966.

Sutcliff, Edmund. *Providence and Suffering in the Old and New Testaments.* London: Nelson, 1953.

Sykes, Stephen. *Sacrifice and Redemption: Durham Essays in Theology.* Cambridge: Cambridge University Press, 1991.

Tautges, Paul. *Comfort the Grieving: Ministering God's Grace in Times of Loss.* Grand Rapids: Zondervan, 2014.

Thrall, Margaret E. *A Critical and Exegetical Commentary on the Second Epistle to the Corinthians.* Edinburgh: Clark, 1994.

Verbrugge, Verlyn, ed. *The NIV Theological Dictionary of New Testament Words.* Grand Rapids: Zondervan, 2000.

Wiersbe, Warren W. *Wiersbe's Expository Outlines on the Old Testament.* Colorado Springs: Cook, 1993.

Worden, J. William. *Grief Counseling and Grief Therapy: A Handbook for the Mental Health Practitioner.* 4th ed. New York: Springer, 2009.

Illustration Credits

CPSIA information can be obtained
at www.ICGtesting.com
Printed in the USA
LVHW081326200523
747529LV00001B/1

9 781662 875366